FROM SEEI

Jennifer Aquilia

ACKNOWLEDGEMENTS
My experience starting a business wouldn't have been so sweet without the friends
who empowered me. From the first photoshoot I was invited to, to the weddings I
was referred, my friends in the industry become Freshly Picked's family. I would like
to make a special thank you to Andi at Andi Mans Photography, Sarah at Sarah
Tucker Events, Josh and Rachel at Best Photography and Erica, my partner in crime.
You encompass grace, talent, and an eye for real beauty.

CONTENTS

An arrangement of carrots, rosemary, fluffy pink peonies and white roses I made in a floral design class in Paris.

1| THE SEED

For me, the start of *Freshly Picked Flowers* was in 2011. I had just graduated with a business degree from the University of Florida, a university that focuses on placing students in corporate jobs and pumping out graduates. It was a place that honored conformity rather than creativity. I was on track to become an accountant. It was in my senior year of college that it hit me: as stable and safe as getting this corporate job seemed, going through with it was like a battle against myself. My ambition and vision to work for myself and cultivate a career in which I could grow as a person was greater than my fear of going nowhere. I decided to ditch the not-so-enticing job offers and follow an entrepreneurial path.

That summer I married my college sweetheart. As I was planning my wedding, I felt like I had entered a different world. A world where self expression was welcomed and celebrated. Where people spent lots of money to enhance the colors and textures and fragrances of a single, cherished day. It seemed like the industry created something that was so real- a product that makes a beautiful impression on peoples lives, very contrary from what I had learned in business school.

With that, I had heightened my creative senses and began to pay attention to my surroundings. What was the most attractive to me was the plant world. It was right there my whole life, yet I had just realized that it was ALIVE. The dancing branches in the trees, the elegantly curling vines, and of course, the darling flowers that bloomed with such grace. This was the start of what I often refer to as my love affair with flowers.

I began to explore anything on the topic of botanics that I could get my hands on. I learned the basics of organic gardening and permaculture design and started a small garden, growing rainbow chard, holy basil, peanuts and potatoes. I adored looking out my window and seeing the bees swarming the fresh buds of the basil, and going outside and seeing the plants growing each day. I took classes on herbalism, healing with plants, and so on. What I was especially drawn to were the more mystical aspects of the plant world, specifically flowers. The way that flowers can treat our emotions with their subtle presence is incredible. I researched Bach Flower Essences and the greater flower essence field on using flowers to heal various emotional conditions. I swooned over flowers everywhere, from the roses in the city gardens, to the budding weeds growing along intersections. I was hooked.

As newlyweds, we decided to take this time when we had no obligations and travel. I saw some of the most beautiful floral terrains. Southern California, Oregon, The Netherlands, and the most impressionable of all: Paris. It was in Paris that I landed in a very small floral design class. There were 3 other students and one inspiring teacher who spoke half the time in French, the other half in English. It was the first experience I had in creating floral arrangements, and I was enthralled. Listening to the teacher, Catherine Muller, as she explained the expressions of each flower and the respective direction they preferred to face, made me realize that I had indeed found my work. I will never forget how it felt to carry my beautiful floral arrangements back to my rental through the streets of Paris at the end of each day. Parisians would stop in their tracks to swoon over my arrangements, and it made my heart sing.

The course lasted four beautiful, dreamy days, and by the end I felt like I had the inspiration I needed to go home and pursue a business in creating floral arrangements.

Your special inspiration is your own seed that will grow into an abundant business if you harness your passion.

I am going to show you exactly how you can start this business with very little money. But what you absolutely cannot lack in is something arguably even more valuable- time. This business will take your full attention to start and even more attention to run. Especially because this formula is for a home based business that is run, at least at first, by solely you. The planning, the sourcing, the marketing, the banking, the booking of the clients, the branding, everything. It will take a lot of time, but what you put into it you will reap in the reward of an engaging, independent, creative outlet that earns you income.

A floral design business is essentially combining an art- floral design- with a perishable product- cut flowers- in a service industry. There is a lot to think about when starting a business in this industry, especially if you are new to the field. My hope is that this book will support you in starting your creative business so you can thrive right off the bat.

LEARNING YOUR CRAFT

Is it necessary to take a class in Floral Design? Well, not exactly. There is no certificate you need to become a florist* and the majority of the design schools in the United States are less than inspiring. However, if you have no experience in floral designing, you will need to spend some time getting a feel for the functionality of various types of arrangements. Let your creativity inspire your designs, but also make sure they are are stable. Practice and work with many styles of flowers and designs before you really start to build a portfolio.

* The state of Louisiana is the only State that does have licensure for florists that all floral designers will need to obtain.

8

Most other 'how to start a business' resources out there will tell you that the first thing you need to do is file to start a company. Well, that is incorrect. The first thing to do is dream up your company name, the image you want to convey, and your overall brand.

Take some time to envision the type of floral business you want to create. There are many floral design businesses out there, so what is it about your business that will make it stand out? What kinds of people do you want your clients to be? Since you are the creative director, the brand will reflect YOU. So think about your own authenticity and your personal style and how you can put that into words.

If the ideas just aren't coming, take some time to relax, sit with some plants, and then let it come to you.

I did this over the course of one week, with pen and paper, jotting down words that came to mind. Ask yourself:

- What words would you use to describe your style?
- What talents set you apart?
- What experiences set you apart?
- What is it that you value in your business?
- What is your twist?
- What flower varieties speak to you?
- What type of clients do you want- wedding clients, commercial, or simply custom orders? Who do you wish to do business with? How do you identify with these people?
- What makes your flowers, your product, different?

- What words resonate with your brand identity?

In meditating over these questions, you will be able to come up with a brand, or identity, and a business name.

Think about how your floral design business name compliments your brand. My company, *Freshly Picked*, was based on a playful and earthy brand. You may want to pick a name that is elegant or traditional, and that is fine. The important thing is that your brand is consistent and authentic.

> **TIP**: Many industry professionals use their personal name for their business, such as *Sarah Sloan Flowers & Styling*. It works great if you have a name that is easy to spell and memorable. The one shortcoming is if you plan to expand and partner up in the future, you may need to go through a name change. Another popular type name is taking two common tools of the trade and placing an & in between, such as *Peony & Twine*, or *Ivy & The Rose*. These are just a couple ideas to help you get started.

DOMAIN + WEBSITE DESIGN

Once you have dreamed up the perfect name and a solid brand, it's time to get to work bringing that dream to reality. You'll want to make sure that your business name is available as a domain online. Sites such as GoDaddy.com and Namecheap.com are where you can purchase your domain for $7-12. If your name isn't available, you can always add a relevant word to the end of your company name, such as 'FreshlyPickedFlowers.com' or 'MoringaFlowersofAustin.com'.

Once you have your domain in your possession, you'll need someone with the technical skills to set you up with a website. The easiest way to get started is to use a WordPress blog that you can build, edit and post to with ease. For your WordPress website design, there are a couple options

> 1- Hire a web designer. This can range in price from a couple hundred to 10K. Personally, I don't think it's necessary and find that the clean and simple designs tend to be more effective in the long run. However this may be a good choice for someone with very little computer skills or time, or if you insist on an elaborately styled website.

> 2- Use a WordPress Theme. This was what I found to be the best way

to go. I found a WordPress theme that was user friendly for about $200. There are many free WordPress themes out there, but I found one with a very good foundation with all the elements I desired. From there I built my site using photoshop and uploaded my images for my logo, photos, and graphics using the simple WordPress theme editor.

TIP: I do not recommend having an intro video or a very graphic intensive website. Mainly, people don't want to watch them and they end up simply taking up space. Also, slow to load internet connections can make the first impression of your website seem choppy and cheap if it has too many elements to load.

Hire a professional to make you an amazing logo.

Your website is usually the first impression your potential clients will have with your brand. That home page will need to capture them and the rest of the website will have to follow through. Each page needs to be professional, interesting, and clean so that your beautiful work can be the main focus that reals them in.

Keep in mind consistency of style throughout your website and even in your emails. Everything from the fonts and logo to the words used will express your quality services.

There are a handful of elements you'll want to make sure you have on your website to make it professional and attractive.

These are the basic pages you will need. Feel free to change around the names to fit your style, but make sure you provide the necessary information.

- *About*
- *Services*
- *Contact*
- *Press*
- *Gallery*
- *Blog, or Homepage*
- and if relevant, a *Shop Now* page

ABOUT YOUR BUSINESS

Here is where you will include a brief summary of your business, what experience you have and who you provide services to. In coming up with this content, ask Yourself: What type of business are you? What do you need your clients to know? What cities do you provide services to? What talents do you have? Why are you a desirable florist?

Stress what makes you different.

And finally, include a bit about the person behind the brand. Take your most wonderful talents and experiences that can show people who you are and express them. Whether you are a passionate botanist, former Anthro employee, or a talented oil painter, these experiences may not seem to directly call to mind floral design but they show your potential clients what you bring to the table.

Example from Freshly Picked:

> *'Freshly Picked is a full service floral design and styling studio servicing Central Florida. We provide flowers for weddings, special events, conventions, styled shoots and more. We love working with clients who appreciate nature, flower varieties that are often overlooked, designs that are simple yet unexpected and romantic style that never fails.*
>
> *'Our philosophy is that the most beautiful blooms are those that are grown with love and a deep respect for the earth. Our flowers are sourced from select flower farms, many of which are local or use sustainable farming methods, ensuring fresh blooms with unique beauty and character.*
>
> *'My experience in floral design is rooted in Paris, where I studied the art of arranging as nature intended; each bloom has it's own personality expressed in shape, color, fragrance and energy.'*

THE SERVICES PAGE

This is as simple as answering the question 'What services do you offer'? Do you intend to offer services for weddings? Single custom arrangements? Prom Corsages? Baby Showers? Restaurant arrangements? Your initial thought may be to offer services to all of the above, in which case you will want to mention each of them so that your potential clients know you can service them properly.

Depending on your target client, you may want to include the prices. For my website, I initially didn't address prices on the website to avoid scaring people off. You also may not know your prices right off the bat, as you'll need to

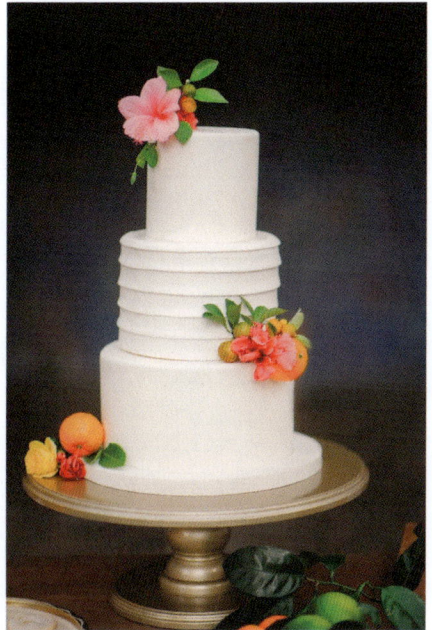

get acquainted with your providers and your desired profit margins. For starting off, I recommend something as simple as:

For a floral design information packet, contact us at info@joeshmoe.com.

or

Custom Wedding Floral Design Packages- email erica@freshflowers.com

Once you get your pricing down, you can say something such as *"Priced from $1000 and vary depending on the varieties, seasonality and scale".*

Example from Freshly Picked:

Wedding Floral Design Packages – *Priced from $1800*

For a wedding floral design information packet, contact us at info@freshlypickedflowers.com.

Botanical Styling for Photo Shoots

Creating a desired look from a blank canvas for photo shoots of all types, from engagement shoots to promotional work. Our styled shoots have been featured on top editorial websites and magazines across the industry.

Florals for Dinner Parties, Bridal Showers, Storefronts, Restaurants, Etc. – *Custom*

A SIMPLE CONTACT PAGE

You want a simple and clear contact page where potential clients can find two things- an email address and a phone number. Your email address will preferably be something along the lines of 'info@yourcompanyname.com' or 'sara@yourcompanyname.com'.

THE PRESS PAGE

This is where potential clients can go to see that yes, you have a good reputation. Since you are probably just getting started and don't have any press, learn how in *Chapter 3 | Time to Sprout.* Once you have been featured in magazines and blogs, have these links available. This also could be a page where you have reviews from past clients.

Your gallery is your portfolio, which should be an ongoing process. These photographs will speak to the client of your style and professionalism so make sure they reflect an image you approve of. Your portfolio is usually the first thing a client looks at to gauge how talented you are, so take it seriously. You want a variety to show your range of skills, but you also need to stay true to your style.

To start, you can comprise it of images you have taken yourself, or have a friend with a nice camera photograph your arrangements.

Your very best images that speak to your brand will be shown in your gallery.

YOUR HOMEPAGE OR BLOG

A very engaging blog will have updated posts about once per week. Articles can be about flower arrangements, events you styled, varieties, clever ideas, or even simply inspiration. The blog will be a main source of traffic to your website. You will be able to share each article through your various social media sources to keep visitors coming back to your website and engaging with you as a professional. If you have a highly engaging blog that reaches your target market correctly, you will become the first floral designer those people think of when they need to order flowers. This is key in establishing yourself in the local community.

I recommend having your homepage actually being a blog, so readers keep coming back to your website and seeing fresh new content. The same page links will always be up top to provide info for interested potential clients. Every time you share a blog post on your social media accounts, viewers will see the homepage of your website and have your information readily available to them.

If your target market includes selling arrangements direct to consumers, you will greatly benefit from having an online and mobile store. Make sure it is simple and clearly priced. One great source for online sales is SquareUp. You can accept credit card payments, process orders, and have a simple store for online and mobile phones made when you create a SquareUp account. You can also look into services such as Shopify to build online retail space. Either way, have your *Shop* page clearly visible for clients who want to buy quickly. Have images of each arrangement and specify flower variety, size, or style of each product. If this is the direction of your flower business, link directly to your *Shop* page as opposed to your homepage when sharing content via social media and advertising platforms.

SOCIAL MEDIA ELEMENTS

One of my main sources of clients was from my Instagram account. I posted beautiful photos of flowers and arrangements everyday and had many industry

professionals and clients get to know me through this means. You will certainly want to use Instagram and have a Facebook page for your business. Both accounts will need a concise bio and an attractive, identifiable image for your profile photo. Use these accounts to connect with other industry professionals as well! Follow them and engage in their posts and they will do the same if you have complimentary style. Post interesting content, beautiful photos and share your excitement for your work.

FILE A COMPANY + OBTAIN PERMITS

Be sure to file your company with the state you will be doing business in and also obtain the appropriate licensing and permits from the state, county and city.

You will need these to open your bank account and to open accounts with wholesalers.

OPEN BANK ACCOUNT

Make it easy on yourself and have one bank account for your business. When you do your books, you will have all your transactions right in front of you. You may set up various streams for obtaining payment from clients that directly go into your bank account: Square, Paypal, and check being the most common. Square is great because you can accept payment over the phone while the client provides their credit card details, or in person with a simple swipe on your phone.

ESTABLISH RELATIONSHIPS WITH FLOWER FARMS + WHOLESALERS

My whole business was focused on sourcing flowers from sustainable and boutique flower farms, so I spent a lot of time researching the best farms and wholesalers. I found that, living in Florida, local flowers were very hard to come by unless they were imported from South America. I ended up finding a handful of great farms around the country that I could rely on and even a wholesaler that sourced from farms that aligned with my vision. The farms you source from will make a big impact on your final product. All flowers are certainly not the same and you will see that even two flowers from the same crop can look very different. I personally love the small, delicate roses that have varying shapes as opposed to stiff roses that are all uniform with each other. I found some small rose gardens with the dreamiest flowers. I also had a couple of local farms

17

I could rely on for accent flowers- snapdragons, eucalyptus, zinnias and belladonna.

It was just a few short weeks into planning out my business that I met a flower farmer named Jim at the local farmers market. I introduced myself and conversed with him about the flower business and my overall vision, how I wanted to source from local farms and have unique, sustainable flowers. By the end of the conversation I had nailed down my first flower source and also made a great connection to the local community. Jim sold flowers through various outlets- from farmers markets to formal farm-to-table dinner events, and I was now his go to for arranging. I ended up arranging flowers at the farmers markets where I made countless connections- from church ministers to event planners to restaurant owners. My first solid connection in business was the least suspecting, but I encourage you to seek out these types of connections by getting out and meeting people face to face. You may use the internet to find flower sources, but don't forget to think outside the box and search farmers markets, local food hubs, industry magazines and flower conventions.

Seasonal and local flowers are the best option both environmentally and for your local community. It's best to try to source from local and regional farms. These farms typically supply a couple varieties of flowers that they specialize in, which means you get flowers that have more character and aren't so common, making your work stand out from the crowd.

Make a list and establish a point of contact at the flower farm. Then setup a corporate account with the farm, allowing you to place orders. That way, when it comes time to make your first flower order, you will be ready. That will be worth your while, so you are not frantically searching for flower farms after booking your first client or photo shoot.

Necessary Supplies and Resources

There are a handful of things that you'll need to successfully run a floral design business. For simplicity, I decided to keep everything as home based as possible. I wasn't at a point where I was able to invest in a cooler, office, and flower truck so I got creative.

All you really need for your office is a laptop, which you probably already have. Maybe a couple folders for organization purposes and a good planner too.

For meetings with clients and partners, you can seek out a local cafe or tea shop that is quiet enough, comfortable, spacious and has wifi. *Chapter 4 | Growth: Booking Clients* has more information on how to make a coffee shop meeting professional.

Here is a simple materials list:
- Floral clippers for hardy stems and branches
- Floral knife- great for quickly trimming thorns off roses and thiner stems
- Twine, ribbons, Raffia, and other materials to wrap flowers that you are drawn to
- An apron to keep the essentials close at hand
- 10-20 large plastic buckets for storing bunches in
- Large and Small mason jars for storing short stemmed flower bunches
- Flower Frogs
- Floral tape
- Floral clay
- Wire in a couple gauges
- Chicken wire

My living room was my flower studio. I had about 10 large plastic buckets from the hardware store for storing flowers in, clippers, a floral knife, lots of twine and waterproof tape. It is important to always use clean, sharp clippers so the flowers have clean healthy cuts and are able to absorb more water. You don't necessarily need flower food. What is even more important is clean water and very clean buckets. You could go as far as using filtered or spring water to ensure your flowers are the healthiest possible. The best temperature to keep cut flowers at is below 65 degrees. When I needed to store flowers, I would turn the air in my house as cold as it would go, bundle up with heavy blankets when I went to sleep and voila, I had a flower cooler. When it was cold outside, I would store flowers in my garage. Just be sure that they are safe from animals, wind, rain, and humidity. I recommend elevating them, even if just on pallets, to protect the flowers from water spillage. You also want to be sure to keep them out of sunlight. For large events I was able to borrow cooler space from the flower farmer I had met.

If you are willing to make the investment, you could buy a flower cooler new or preferably second hand, and have it set up in a garage or outdoor shed. An even better option in the beginning phases of your company is to find a business owner who may have extra cooler space that you can rent from them.

It's also a great way to get your product visible to more potential clients. Do make sure that your flowers are stored nowhere near fruits and vegetables which may shorten their vase life.

I didn't have a flower truck, but I did have a friend with an SUV and that was all I needed. I would load up the SUV real safe and secure with flower arrangements for my gigs, turn the air all the way down and drive very slowly to my destination. For very large weddings I would rent a sprinter van that was large enough to transport tall arrangements.

Eventually, I connected with a boutique grocery store owner that let me use their cooler space as well. So seek out various business owners that may have coolers and see if you can rent space from them. It's less expensive then buying a cooler, especially because you would most likely need to also rent a studio to house the cooler.

The largest investment you will need to make upfront will be in building your portfolio, which we will get to next!

3 | TIME TO SPROUT

'Walk with the dreamers, the believers, the courageous, the cheerful, the planners, the doers, the successful people with their heads in the clouds and their feet on the ground. Let their spirit ignite a fire within you to leave this world a better than when you found it.'
-WILFERD PETERSON

It starts with creating content to share with the world. You may not have professional photos of your work but don't let that hold you back in the least. When I created my online presence, it was completely comprised of photos I had taken myself of foraged neighborhood flowers. Some with my Canon digital camera, others simply with my iPhone. Being a pro photographer is not necessary, you just need a good eye and a love for creating arrangements. If you stay true to your style you will begin to gather a following organically. And the content you create doesn't all need to be arrangements. Any content of a related subject with your perspective is part of your image. Basically, share your love, your excitement, your adoration, and other like minded people will want to work with you. Why? Because they started out like you, and they still have that spark that makes them unique and successful.

Some of my first blog posts didn't have flower arrangements in them at all. I talked about flower symbolism, about the magic of flowers, and my floral philosophy.

'The sweet fragrance and undeniable beauty of flowers has gotten them well deserved attention in every culture throughout history. While they are pleasing to the eye, their purpose is much greater than providing ambiance. Flowers are nature's most beautiful work, and bring us bliss, happiness, gratitude, and energy. We learn from flowers. They teach us about the cycle of life, to appreciate the senses, and much more on a deeper level.'

23

I also posted extensively on flowers I discovered during my travels. I shared photos and epiphanies. Sights and scents of the delicate peonies and garden roses at the Parisian flower markets, the happy wildflowers along the mediterranean coast, the inspiring visit to Claude Monet's gardens in Giverny, and even the arrangements I made in my floral design class.

'Claude Monet's gardens are in the small village of Giverny, just a little outside of Paris. These lush gardens are where Monet gained inspiration for many of his most famous paintings, and they have been restored and kept up for those also seeking inspiration, as well as endless amounts of excited schoolchildren and agitated tourists. Despite the crowds and the cold rain, the garden was magnificent. The rain almost made the gardens even more beautiful. They convey the epitome of french garden style; incorporating seasonal flowers and harmonious colors, and allowing mother nature to grow without interference, restoring the old instead of building new, and focusing on the charm of the moment, which will look different every day as new flowers bloom and old ones mature. It's whimsical, nostalgic, and fresh at the same time.'

After months of creating content, contacting professionals to engage in working together was the natural next step. Your goal is to get your foot in the door, to be involved in their projects and photo shoots.

Now it's time to create a list of your dream team, those professionals whose work your love and that you would love to work with.

Remember when you thought of the type of clients you want to book? What photographers, wedding planners, and caterers do they hire? Where do they book their wedding venue? What bridal salons will they be shopping in? Also, who in your industry inspires you? Whose style do you feel is similar to yours? Who is getting published? Who do you wish to work with?

Here are the different types of industry professionals to consider.

- Photographers
- Wedding Planners
- Caterers
- Wedding Cake Bakers
- Bridal Salon Owners
- Wedding Venue Managers
- Restaurant and Bar Owners
- Boutiques Managers
- Hotel Managers

Keep in mind that the networking you do is the most constructive aspect of building your company. These established vendors will be your 'in' to booking your first of many clients.

Content and an online presence are one thing, but real life gigs- photo shoots, events, etc, will need to be in your portfolio before a total stranger will give you money for your services. You may be lucky enough to have a family friend who is willing and trusting to hire you with no prior professional floral experience, and if you do then take the opportunity. If you don't have those opportunities, then you'll have to plan some amazing photo shoots.

Take the list you made of industry professionals and begin to reach out to them. This can be accomplished subtly and with taste. Follow and engage with them on social media, share your passion and likewise and you'll see them begin to notice and engage back with you. Reach out to the ones you feel most connected with and introduce yourself, offer to supply them with complementary arrangements for a photo shoot or for their office. You can even go as far as offering to help them with their gigs, to get a taste of the industry.

Before you know it, one of them will reach out to you for your first gig. It will most likely be unpaid- maybe a shoot for an editorial, a sample arrangement or a fun promotional photoshoot. I mentioned that you can start this home based floral business with very little startup cost. But that doesn't mean free. If you want to impress, you'll eventually need more flowers than what your neighborhood front yards can supply. You'll have to go to the grocery stores, wholesalers, or local flower farms and buy flowers for your portfolio that you are building. And when you begin the networking and offering to share your work, you are going to be doing it for free. Compared to other startup business plans, a $50, $200 or even $500 cost for a photo shoot that will get your business off the ground isn't so bad.

I had been blogging and creating content for months when I reached out to a handful of wedding planners and film photographers. Before I knew it, I was invited to be a part of a photo shoot for *The Everygirl* with *Sarah Tucker Events*. It was a photo shoot for an end of summer party, and it was my first time ordering flowers and having them shipped in for a project! I paid for the flowers, my hotel and travel costs out of pocket. I was excited and nervous as I eagerly awaited the big box of flowers to show up, at my hotel room no less. I knew when I saw the bellhop carrying the box on its side, blatantly ignoring the 'this side up' warning, that the flowers may not be in pristine condition. And then I opened them. Every single rose, hydrangea and peony were wilted and brown. The August Florida sun had got them good. Somehow, I was left with a couple of bunches of ranunculus, anemones, and some accent florals to create 5 arrangements in large chinoiserie vases. I was on the verge of panicking when I realized that I had to figure something out.

More often than not, the flowers come and they are less than perfect. Occasionally, they come and they are destroyed. You have to be prepared for these circumstances, emotionally and logistically, and find a way to overcome

without causing a panic. You have to be able to figure out how you can, despite the circumstances, use what you have to make a final product that is beautiful and that will align with the client's vision. I stayed calm and the outcome was arrangements that were rather unique, and apparently very beautiful.

They ended up getting published on *The Everygirl* as planned, and shortly afterwards, I booked my first client.

How to Organize a Photo Shoot

The best way to build your portfolio from scratch is by organizing photo shoots with industry professionals. This is the fun part! You can dream up the most creative, expressive vision and bring it to life with other industry professionals.

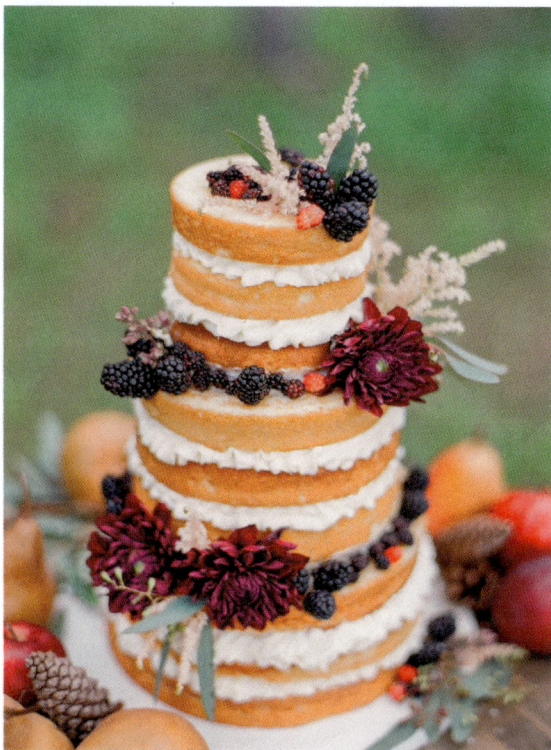

The most important elements to your photo shoot are your arrangements and having a talented photographer to capture them. It is even better if you have curated details: models in costume, a killer venue, a tasteful tablescape and unique paper products. The point of the shoot is not only to get your portfolio built, but it is also a fantastic way to get published and start building your reputation.

Getting published not only gets your name out there to clients and other vendors, but it also shows potential clients that you are professional and trustworthy, not to mention that your work is beautiful.

Some Keys to Making the Most of your Photo Shoots

- Include lots of details. From the paper products to the napkins, vases, boutonnieres, and chair garlands. And each detail needs to be consistent in style, unpredictable and lovely.
- Work with professionals. Especially those who have been published before!
- Go all out on the florals. Make your most beautiful work stand out!
- Use a Pinterest board to organize your vision and have everyone involved collaborate on the board too.
- Have a schedule and give yourself extra time.

- Take lots of photos for social media (Instagram, Facebook, and your blog). Even though the photographer is shooting, it's a great way to market yourself with your behind the scenes shots.
- Source vases from thrift stores, antique shops, craft stores and the like.

When the shoot is complete and the images are ready, it's time to send them away to publishers. The easiest way to get published is online via an industry blog. For the wedding industry, *Style Me Pretty*, *Wedding Chicks*, and *Grey Likes Weddings* are the top wedding blogs. Also consider local blogs and even local magazines. When you send out your shoot, include as much content as possible and all of the relevant vendor information.

If and when you eventually get published, make sure to share it on your blog and social media accounts.

Make sure your photoshoots are authentic, unique and have a storyline with attention to detail.

When you begin to have potential clients contact you, the face of your company is as important as everything you have built up thus far. How you respond in emails, phone calls, answering machines and how you appear in meetings will speak volumes about your professionalism.

Many of your potential clients will initially contact you via email. That being said, it is important to respond to every client email within 48 hours. The client needs to feel important and you also have a short window of interest before they find a different florist. And respond with enthusiasm and personality. Don't be bland for the sake of professionalism, but of course be extremely polite.

The same goes for phone calls. I recommend scheduling phone consultations so that you can be sure to have a quiet environment to talk in and so that you can give the phone call your full attention.

During this phase of booking your first clients, I recommend setting an appointment to meet in person if possible. I would meet at a teahouse or cafe in town that was close in proximity to the client and aligned with their style. It is more professional than having a potential client come to your home, even if you have a nice home office set up. Whichever way you end up performing the initial consultation, be prepared. Have their vision board ready and think of some unique flower varieties to recommend. Bring images of your work, inspirational visuals, and a notebook for digging into details. Get familiar with their venue and any other details they have already planned. Have unique ideas ready to share for their arrangements, and even a couple price points. They will be asking a lot of questions, so try to anticipate these questions and have answers ready. Such as- How much do you charge for delivery? How much time will you need to set up? Do Peonies bloom in June? How do you describe your style? What are your fees?

The art of closing will transition throughout your business life. At this point, closing during the consultation is not necessary and can even be difficult. The point of the consultation is to gather all the information you need to make your potential client's quote. When the meeting is coming to an end, wrap it up and let the client know to expect your quote in the mail (or email) within 5 business days along with a contract.

Let them know that if they decide to hire you upon reading the quote, they simply need to print, sign and mail in the contract and pay a specified deposit. Also give them all of your information, again, and remind them that they can contact you with any questions, additional details or comments. Oh, and pay for their drink!

Then, go home and make their quote.

ELEMENTS OF THE QUOTE

The client's quote will need all of the relevant information as well as plenty of inspirational photos in an organized and easy to understand manner. Remember, they are probably going to be receiving quotes from several different florists, so make yours beautiful and detailed to stand out.

A great format is as follows:

Company Logo
Client Name
Event Date
Venue
Event City
Inspiration: Colors, styles, themes
Botanical Elements: Flower varieties

This is a great space to include inspirational photos, but you may also include them throughout the quote to get your vision across.

Break the Floral Elements Down by section. For example:

Ceremony
Cocktail Hour
Reception
Fees (Delivery, Set, Strike)

Then, in each section, have the elements listed by name with the price and a description. At the end, include a price breakdown with sales tax and the deposit due now to reserve the date. Save it as a .pdf and share it with the potential client.

SIMPLE FLOWER PRICING FORMULA:

1. List out the requested floral elements and the flowers, vases and supplies needed to create those arrangements.
2. Create a list of the costs you will incur to fill the order. You can get flower prices from your flower source. Remember to order a little bit extra flowers in case of spoiling. Calculate the total expenses, including shipping. Multiply it by 2.
3. This number, plus sales tax, will be the Client's total price.
4. Price the elements on the quote accordingly so they all add up to your final number. Assign a price to each element in a way that it makes sense and

they all add up to the correct total. Include fees such as delivery, set-up, etc.

FLOWER PRICING EXAMPLE

1 |
Small Ceremony Flower Order

Item	Estimated Flowers Necessary	Other Supplies
Bridal Bouquet	5 Peonies, 5 Garden roses, 4 ranunculus, 1 bunch jasmine vine, 1 bunch maiden hair fern, 1 hydrangea	White Silk Ribbon
Bridesmaid Bouquets(3)	6 Peonies, 9 Garden roses, 9 ranunculus, 1 bunch seeded Eucalyptus	Raffia
Boutonniere's (5)	5 succulents, 7 blue thistle	Raffia, Boutonniere Pins
Cocktail Tables (20)	30 Garden Roses	7 Small brass vases

2 |
Total Costs:

11 Peonies- 3 Bunches (They come in bunches of 5, so order 3 bunches to have a couple extra)	$32*3
44 Garden Roses- 4 Bunches (Come in bunches of 12 from our supplier)	$45*4
13 Ranunculus- 2 Bunches	$18*2
1 Bunch Jasmine Vine	$8.50
1 Bunch Maiden Hair Fern	$12
1 Bunch Hydrangea	$36
7 Succulents (Order a couple extra)	$3.25*7
1 Bunch Blue Thistle	$12.50
Boutonniere Pins	$3.50
20 Small Brass Vases	$150
Raffia	$5
White Silk Ribbon	$7
Shipping costs for flowers	$170

Total Expenses	$739.25
	x2
Client's subtotal:	$1,478.50

3 |
Add Sales Tax

Total Price * 1.0+Sales Tax Rate
Sales tax rate of 6.5%:
1478.5*1.065= $1574.60 — Client's Final Price

4 |
Price Quote Accordingly

Bridal Bouquet		175
Bridesmaid Bouquets (3)70		210
Boutonniere's (5) 18		90
Cocktail Tables (20)43		860
Fees:		
Delivery		100
Set		45
subtotal		$1,480
+.065% sales tax		96.2
Total Price		$1,576.20

*Note: the numbers don't have to be exact. It's fine to round up to the next dollar to make your numbers easier.

This will become easier the more you do it, and overtime you will even come up with consistent prices such as Bridal Bouquet: $150, Boutonniere: $20.

With this formula, you will have profit margins of about 50%. So if you sign a $1000 event, you'll make $500 profit. These are very good margins for a startup business! And even better, your client pays their final balance before you order the flowers, so there is very minimal financial risk.

The average floral cost for a wedding is $1000-2500, but that can depend on your market.

> **TIP:** What makes this business have such little startup cost is scheduling your payments as such:
> **Have a $300 deposit to book with you, and the remaining final balance due one month before the event. This will give you enough time to order the**

flowers without paying anything out of pocket.

The Contract

The contract is the document that promises your services to the client, and the clients payment to you for those services. Include relevant contact information for the client and you, as well as deposits, amounts due and dates. You may hire a lawyer to write your contract, or you could simply use one you find online as a guide, and adapt it to your business where necessary.

Accepting Payment

The easiest ways to accept payment is check, but that isn't always convenient for the client. You can easily download a Square Ap and create an online and mobile store where you may create personalized 'items' such as 'Deposit' or 'Remaining Balance' for your clients to check out. Another simple way to accept payment is via Paypal.

Invoices are typically necessary for business clients, but occasionally personal clients will request them as well. An invoice simply needs the following information: The company name and contact info, the details of the items ordered such as price, description and quantity, any delivery information, a price breakdown with a final amount due and the date.

You'll want to have a signed contract with the initial payment, so the most common method for your first payment is check. When the due date for the final payment is approaching, send an email or a phone call to remind the client.

> **TIP:** If possible, save 10-20% of your profit from each event to invest back into your business. That way, you will be able to finance future business growth with the clients you book upfront and won't need to pay anything out of your own pocket or take out loans.

Closing

How do you close a client? Especially, your first client? The answer is in the effort and energy you show them from the beginning. Responding to emails, phone calls, and sharing inspiration with them on social media from the get go will impress them greatly. Being excited about their event, their inspiration, and showing that in your quote with vivid details and beautiful images will blow them away. Finally, top it all off with professionalism and confidence, know that you have your business together and simply offer this:

'After receiving the flower proposal, there is a $300 deposit that reserves your wedding date with Freshly Picked.'

or

'Should you proceed and hire us for your event, please send the signed contract and deposit to (insert address)'.

It will get easier and easier as you gain experience and a good reputation. Expect some back and forth with the client after they receive their quote and before they book, as they will have a lot of questions and may want to make changes to the quote. Again, respond promptly and with enthusiasm and they will feel confident in hiring you.

CLIENT RELATIONSHIP

The client relationship is huge, almost as important as your flower work. How you make them feel and perceive your business will make or break your success. For your first meeting, you could bring them a stem of your favorite flower for the client as inspiration. When you mail out your signed contract, include a small, thoughtful and pretty gift. Remember, this is a very special occasion to your clients and it is your job to bring their dreams to life.

The more involved you become with your client's creative process, the **better your business will do.**

Your drive for an impeccable event will show through your portfolio, as each and every image will convey the gorgeous attention to detail and cohesiveness of your projects. Discussing elements beyond the florals is something that will separate you from the rest of the florists. Give your clients golden ideas and inspiration and they will rave about you, as will the other vendors involved in the event.

The client will already have in their mind that you put your full attention and energy into their order, and all you have to do on the day of is follow through. If your relationship with your client is less than awesome, minor snafus will be blown out of proportion and could hurt any chance of a referral, positive review and just be an emotional blow.

A great tool for the creative process is *Pinterest*, an online image gathering website that you can collaborate with clients and other vendors on to share inspiration. This is a great way for clients to share with you what they do and do not love, for you to show them interesting flower varieties and ideas, and for ideas to bloom. It will keep your visions aligned and it's really fun!

I also suggest having a physical inspiration board that is complete with the client's information, a color chart, samples of fabrics, photos of arrangements and flower varieties, and any other element that will go into the project. It's great for organizing creative ideas and concepts, and the final board will be extremely helpful when you are preparing for the day of the project, while you order flowers, purchase supplies, and of course during the time you spend arranging the flowers.

If you really want to go above and beyond to wow your clients, bring your inspiration board to client meetings (even an initial inspiration board for your first consultation) or mail them an image rich copy.

As you work through the creative process on a flower order, keep your notes extremely organized and updated so that you will be prepared for making your flower order and then arranging the flowers.

ORDERING THE FLOWERS

Once you receive the final payment from the client, you are ready to order flowers for the event!

Take the various flower sources you have in your database and contact them to see who has the best varieties of the various flowers you will need.

Envision the arrangements you will be making and what flowers will go into them. It is hard to estimate how many of each variety you will need, and there is no magic number. Even flowers of the same variety come in all shapes and sizes, so it is best to order extra in case some are smaller than expected. You also want to order more than you think you'll need in case some are spoiled, and there are always a couple bunches that are.

Flowers that will be shipped in to you will be overnighted, usually via FedEx. I highly recommend having the flowers arrive 2 days before the event! That gives you one day to prep, and one day to arrange. Also, if there is a delay in shipping and they arrive a day late, you would be out of luck if you only ordered them one day in advance. This does happen, quite frequently. I have had flowers get lost and arrive a day late on multiple occasions, and giving myself an extra day was always what saved the day.

VASES AND VESSELS

The vases you use will vary per client. I found that collecting vases on a per event basis was quite effective. For my very first client, I used a mixture of vases she provided and bought some from boutiques and craft stores. Each event your collection will grow. I suggest factoring in the costs of inexpensive vases into your client's quote. If you want to add some expensive vases to your collection, you could consider them an investment and only charge your client a small rental fee. The same goes for props such as arbors, chuppahs and pedestals.

I avoid using flower foam at all costs. It is very toxic and it constricts the design of the flowers. I would much rather use some chicken wire mashed up in a vase or a flower frog glued down to the center of a vase. They will allow your designs to breathe and have more flow.

Floral Design Concepts

Your personal style will develop the more you work with flowers. Look at other designs for inspiration, but only inspiration and not to try to imitate. There are many styles out there, each can be beautiful and there is room for you to dream up your own designs for a unique product.

The wonderful thing about the floral industry is there is no standardized test to pass. Your floral designs don't need to meet any specific requirement. Its important however, that your style is consistent and your designs are functional. You don't want flowers falling off of the chuppah during the ceremony!

Some basic floral design concepts to inspire your work!

Boutonnieres

My favorite boutonnieres are made using unexpected plants and textures. I love getting creative with succulents, dried flowers and pods. My recipe for boutonnieres is one focal element, an accent and some foliage. I don't use glue, just tightly wrapped twine and occasionally floral tape. I like to finish with ribbon, burlap, velvet, or raffia. Make sure to have extra boutonniere pins on hand! Boutonnieres are around $16 each.

Flower Crowns

What could signify a sense of occasion more than wearing flowers in your hair? What could be more feminine and beautiful? I love creating floral crowns because they're graceful yet so primitive. With flower crowns remember, bigger is not better. A simple vine such as jasmine or ivy along with some small roses is my favorite. Crowns can be time consuming to create, so price a little more for these. My favorite type of flower crown is a foliage dense vine- ivy and smilax are beautiful- as a base. They can be taped with green floral tape in the back to hold their shape. Then simply add flowers with the green floral tape. For crowns without foliage, I suggest heavy twine for a base and then adding the flowers from there.

Top: A crown of ivy and garden grown roses

Right: A crown of dried lavender

*A simple smilax crown adorned with fresh blooms and buds of
Elderberry*

Bouquet

The bridal bouquet our favorite. Bridal bouquets are usually around $150. Our bouquet style is romantic, natural and free yet elegant. I adore mixing vines, ferns or ivy with the fluffiest peonies and garden roses, and always add some sweet pea, lilac or maidenhair fern to soften it. My favorite technique for a bridal bouquet is a loose hand tied or spiral construction, and adding fluffy foliage and accents to the edges to soften the shape. Go with your own style and remember to finish the stems with a clean cut!

Centerpieces

Centerpieces should be low enough for guests to see over but still make a visual impact. We use a couple focal flowers, accents and lots of greens to make our centerpiece arrangements lush. Make each one a little different by playing with the shape and don't forget to polish the vases.

6| A BEAUTIFUL HARVEST

PREP THE SPACE

For weddings and large orders, your manual prep begins three days before the event. You will want to clean and prepare your studio space for the flowers to come in. Have everything as organized as possible so you will have an efficient work flow. Have your buckets scrubbed clean with hot water, soap and bleach. Fill them all with water so you can immediately get to hydrating the flowers when they arrive the following day. Double check that you have all your supplies, vases, inspiration board and two copies of the flower order.

PREP THE FLOWERS

Two days before the event, your flowers should arrive. Upon receiving the box, check that you have all the flowers ordered and that they are in good condition. Report to your account representative any issues with the flowers. Then, it's time to get to work!

Put all the flowers by bunch in water. I recommend trimming the stems first, so they have a clean cut and are able to soak up more water. You also want to cut off any foliage below the water line, as they can cause bacteria in the water. Use clean water, preferably filtered or spring, and if you like, a basic professional flower preservative to prolong their vase life. When all the flowers are in the buckets of water, store them in a cool space under 65 degrees and protected from breeze, humidity and sunlight.

Reorganize the space and make sure everything is in place for arranging the flowers.

If Your Flower Shipment is Delayed

Occasionally you may find yourself in an unfortunate scenario in which your shipment doesn't arrive on the expected day. Overnighted shipments that are delayed typically arrive the following day, but be ready in case they are spoiled, lost, or have further delays. Some backup sources you can rely on are local flower wholesalers, grocery stores, local flower farms, plant nurseries, and neighborhood gardens.

The day before the event is when you will arrange the flowers. All the prep you did the previous two days will pay off in the time you are now able to put into arranging.

For weddings, I like to start with the bouquets, because those are what will be seen the most and you'll want to use the healthiest and prettiest flowers in the bouquets.

While arranging, keep in mind that the flowers will open up a bit before the event, so leave some room for them to bloom.

I also recommend adding the finishing touches, such as the ribbons and twine and boutonniere pins, the day of.

Arranging the flowers takes a long time, usually 12+ hours! But it's important to have all the arrangements complete so that you can spend all your energy delivering, setting up and dealing with the client on the big day.

THE DAY OF

The big day is finally here! Setup for events is usually two hours before, but I would give yourself double that for your first couple of events until you have a good gauge on how long it takes you.

The day of your first big event can be pretty intimidating. Remember that you have prepared as much as possible and your client wouldn't have hired you if they didn't already love your work!

When you see your clients, make sure to congratulate them and try to appear calm! If you seem rushed or nervous they will feed off of that energy. Try to make the majority of your communication with the catering manager or the event planner.

Once you have everything set up, do a run through to make any changes or final touches. I like to pull off aging petals and arrange a flower here and there. Also, make sure to get photos! Your phone or a small point and shoot camera will suffice, as you don't want to lug around a large camera or piss off the photographer. Share your work on social media, and tag the other vendors you are working with as well as the location!

Before you leave, double check with the planner that they don't need anything else from you and then head out!

Sometimes, you may feel like you are running out of time. There was one wedding where I was tying the aisle florals to the pews when I realized the guests were arriving! In this scenario you'll have to make a quick executive decision to continue and finish the job or get out of there. In this case, I had an angry church wedding coordinator giving me the look, so I knew it was time to abandon ship.

If you are returning to strike, be sure to return at the specified time and collect all your arrangements.

FOLLOW UP

For small orders such as cafe arrangements, a simple email or phone call will do. For larger clients, send a note or even a small gift of congratulations. If they respond complimenting your work, follow up with a link for the client to leave a review if you have any account with Yelp, WeddingWire, or other review websites.

In about a month, the photographer should have the completed photographs ready. If they do not contact you, reach out to them and request photos for use on your website.

Another point of followup communication you will need to make is with your flower supplier. As you build your relationship with them, it is always good to get in touch with them and let them know your thoughts on the flower order and any comments you need to make. It is especially important to let them know of any issues with the flowers, such as spoilage upon arrival or especially short vase life. This way you can be properly refunded.

After you have about 10 big events or clients in your portfolio, you are ready to really grow your business. You are at the point where you feel comfortable meeting new clients, dealing with the creative process and executing the day of. Now is when the business really takes off!

As your time becomes more valuable, you'll get to a point where you stop doing things for free. Even collaborative photo shoots don't have to be unpaid. Get creative with your team and find advertisers, magazines, and venues who you can pitch an idea for a photo shoot to.

CHOOSING YOUR CLIENTS

Some components of your strategy will change as you generate more business. You might feel the need to hire help, alter your pricing, and choose your clients differently. That's right, choose your clients. Because when you get to the point where you are getting inquiries everyday, you will be able to pick and choose your clients just as they choose you! At this point, it's likely that you've experienced pesky clients, or the unmentionable bridezilla (or worse, momzilla!) or even personalities that just don't jam well with you. It's important to learn to identify the unwanted clients early on and politely cut communication.

One characteristic I wasn't particularly fond of was the controlling client. The bride that has charts of every table, with a diagram showing where each and every vase should be exactly placed, leaving absolutely no room for creativity. I learned to avoid booking with these type of clients by looking for overly controlling personalities in the consultation and politely explaining that we were not available any longer in the follow up communication.

Some pesky client personality types are unforeseeable. I had one client that was as sweet as could be for the entire process, and I was so excited to present her flowers to her as they were some of my favorite arrangements to date. When she called me the next day to criticize the flowers being of 'low quality' and that they ruined her day, I was speechless. Well, following the event they happened to be featured on the homepage of *StyleMePretty.com* and I could see in the photographs that they were in fact, gorgeous. I realized that you can't always take criticisms from clients personally, especially not when they seem irrational to you. Understand that clients may be under a lot of stress and their method of unleashing that stress may happen to fall upon you, and it happens.

To Grow or To Stabilize?

At this point in your business, you will need to decide whether or not you wish to take your business to the next level, or to simply keep it at the level it is at. At this point I was bringing in a good side income, about $2k per month with an average of 2 events and a handful of small orders each month. I was at a point where I could either stabilize my business and continue to let it run as it was, or to grow it.

If you want your business to flourish and provide you with an income you can thrive on, here are some tips to take it to that level.

Hire Help

You'll get inquiries for larger orders and begin to feel like you need to hire help to service these big orders. You'll also be able to book more than one client per weekend, or even per day. Lets say you book one wedding every weekend during wedding season. If you had one employee, you would be able to book multiple events in a weekend. This not only doubles your business, but it increases your margins because you can order more flowers together in bulk, use the same delivery van if you are renting one, etc.

It also allows you to be able to do more of what you love- the arranging- while your employee can focus on the delivering, the packing, the prepping, and so on.

I recommend hiring slowly and with a lot of thought going into who you choose to hire. Pick someone who is creative and talented, a hard worker, and that has a friendly attitude. You can choose to hire by the hour or per event. Either way, make sure you abide by employment laws and pay the appropriate taxes. Also, make sure you are still making a profit with your employees factored in.

INVEST IN EQUIPMENT

If you feel like your business growth is being held back by a lack of equipment, space, or professional vehicle, then it's time to consider investing. You may use the 10-20%   you saved from your profits to purchase what will allow your business to grow. Depending on where you live, you may be able to have a cooler in your garage or home studio. If not, you'll need to start finding a space that is a good location and price for your new studio home. This will also be a place where you can host consultations, flower arranging classes, flower parties, and whatever other dreamy projects you can come up with. Also keep in mind the location of your spot and what other business are around you. It might be good to score a location next to a wedding planning studio, a bridal boutique, an invitation shop, or a bakery.

If you are looking for a cooler, be sure to check second hand sources such as CraigsList and Ebay. Also, be sure to get a cooler that is suitable for flowers, as the humidity can differ.

ADVERTISING

In the startup phase, advertising is not so effective. But once you have built a reputation and experience, it will probably be something you want to consider utilizing. The most relevant advertising streams for this industry are print and online.

PRINT

Print advertising includes bridal magazines, community newspapers, niche magazines such as the 'Edible' series for farm-to-vase type companies, or local luxury magazines for high end florists. The most value for your advertising dollar in print will be achieved if you focus on location. There is not much use in advertising yourself in a nationwide publication if your target market is just in your city. Seek out city, state, and regional publications to get your name out there.

INTERNET

The power of the internet makes advertising easy, inexpensive and highly targeted. There are a handful of places you can advertise online, the best ones being Google, industry blogs, and Facebook. I found advertising on Facebook to be very easy and I saw quick results.

ADVERTISE ON FACEBOOK

The advertising system in Facebook is pretty straightforward, but here are some tips to get you started.

- Set your target market to be a specific audience. For a wedding florist you may target engaged women, age range of 21-40, with college degrees and with a particular income. You can even target based on keywords they may like; 'Southern Weddings', 'StyleMePretty', or even target those who 'like' your competitors.
- Make the content of your ad one big, beautiful image that conveys your very best work, a simple headline and a brief ad copy explaining what you offer. Such as *'Locally sourced floral design based in Winter Park, Fl'* or *'Not Your Mother's Wedding Flowers. Inquire today!'* Make your ad a good representation of your overall brand and personality.
- Have the link of the ad go to a page on your website, preferably a blog post showcasing your best work.
- Make sure your website is up to date and has a clear point of contact and information about your services.
- You may also run a 'like' campaign, in which you advertise your business Fanpage on Facebook in order to build your page's 'likes'. It helps to make your business look reputable when prospective clients are researching their options.

I used only two channels for advertising- Southern Weddings (print and online) and Facebook ads, and they were both extremely effective in different ways. The Southern Weddings advertising got me some inquiries, but the real value was in the reputation it gave me to say that we were a Southern Weddings approved vendor. The Facebook advertisements brought me a constant stream of inquiries.

Other means of getting your business out to the public without spending dollars on advertising are via your social media outlets. Instagram probably brought me more clients than any other source. Pinning your work on Pinterest, engaging with your co-venders and clients via Instagram and Facebook and keeping a beautiful, active blog will generate many booked clients.

Your business will advance to the next level when you have the infrastructure in place to take in larger orders and more of them, as well as a consistent, beautiful presence online and in print.

Right when *Freshly Picked* was up and running, with multiple inquiries and bookings coming in per week, was when I gave birth to my first child. Naturally I wanted all of my energy to go into taking care of my baby, and I decided to slow down with the flower business. It was in perfect timing when Erica, a brilliant, hardworking gal who knew the botanical world inside and out popped up with a desire to work with flowers. She became my partner in crime and shortly after learning the ropes went on to run the business herself. Her love of arranging flowers and being in the industry is what inspired me write this book, hoping that many more like her will be empowered to do the same.

8 | RESOURCES

BASIC WEDDING OR EVENT TIMELINE

	Task	Response Time
Inquiry	Contact client to set up consultation	Within 24 Hours
Consultation	Meet with client and dream up their flower order	When scheduled
Respond with Pitch	Send Quote and Contract to Client	Within 3 Business Days
Client Researches Options	Respond to all questions and comments from client on their quote or contract	Immediately
Client Hires Your Business: Pays Deposit and Sends Contract	Send email to confirm payment, attach signed contract and thank them for their business!	Within 24 Hours
The Creative Process with Client	Collaborate and keep in touch on the creative process. Keep notes on numbers and flower varieties for your flower order and any supplies necessary	Continually until the event. Always respond to all emails and phone calls within 24 hours.
Final Payment	Send email requesting final balance	1 Month Before Event
Confirmation	Send email confirming payment received and thanking them for their business	Immediately following payment

Order Flowers	Order flowers to arrive 2 days before the event	Immediately following payment. At least 3 weeks before event.
Gather Supplies	Have all supplies purchased and gather all non floral elements you may need	2 weeks before event
Prep Studio Space	Have your flower arranging station set up with clean buckets, organized supplies, inspiration board up and ready and a clean, good energy space!	3 days before event
Flowers Arrive!	Prep flowers and hydrate them. Keep them in a cool, dry place out of sunlight.	2 days before event
Arrange all flowers!	Arrange all of the beautiful flowers and get everything in place for delivery the following day.	Day before event

Deliver	Add all final touches to arrangements and floral elements. Pack the truck and deliver and set up for the event, and strike at the end of the event if it is included in your contract. Share behind the scene details on social media.	Day of event
Follow up	Send a note or maybe a small gift of congratulations! Don't talk specifically about the flowers, but the day. If they respond complimenting your work, follow up with a link for the client to leave a review.	Following week
Obtain photos	Request photographs from photographer and add them to your portfolio.	Following month

RECOMMENDED CLASSES
Little Flower School
New York City
www.littleflowerschoolbrooklyn.com

Catherine Muller
Paris
www.catherinemuller.com

SUPPLIERS
Florabundance Wholesaler
Carpinteria, California
www.florabundance.com

Peterkort Roses
Portland, Oregon
www.peterkortroses.com

Roseville Farms
Central Florida
www.rosevillefarms.com

Locally Grown Flowers
Sanford, Florida
407.284.9481

Photography Credits

Cover	Andi Mans Photography, www.andimansphotography.com
1	Jessica Lorren Organic Photography, www.jessicalorren.com
4	Jennifer Aquilia
6	Jennifer Aquilia
7	Best Photography, www.bestphotographyfl.com
8	Best Photography
9	Andi Mans Photography
11	Logo by Juliet Grace Design, www.julietgracedesign.com
12	Jennifer Blair Photography, www.jenniferblairphotography.com
13	Best Photography
15	Andi Mans
16	Jennifer Aquilia
17	Jennifer Aquilia
18	Jennifer Aquilia
19	Jennifer Blair
22	Best Photography
23	Jennifer Aquilia (Both)
24	Jennifer Aquilia
25	Andi Mans
27	Naomi Chokr Photography, www.naomichokr.com
28	Best Photography
29	Best Photography
30	Best Photography (Both)
31	Jessica Lorren
32	Kismis Ink, www.kismisink.com
38	Shannon Kirsten, www.shannonkirsten.com
39	Shannon Kirsten
41	Jessica Lorren
42	Jessica Lorren (Top), Kismis Ink (Bottom Left) Jennifer Blair (Bottom Right)
43	Best Photography (Both)
44	Jennifer Aquilia (Top), Best Photography (Bottom)
45	Best Photography
46	Best Photography (Top Left, Top Center), Andi Mans (Top Right), Jason Mize, www.jasonmizephotography.com (Bottom Left), Jennifer Blair (Bottom Right)
47	Best Photography
48	Kismis Ink
49	Shannon Kirsten
50	Best Photography (Both)
51	Andi Mans
52	Andi Mans
54	Jennifer Aquilia

Printed in Great Britain
by Amazon